THE SCERET OF A HAPPY MARRIAGE

A Peaceful and Happy Home

Onyimon

Dedicated to my lovely husband and my three darling sons. You guys make my world complete. You all give me nothing but joy, love and happiness.

"A GREAT MARRIAGE does not happen because of the love you had in the beginning but how well you continue building love until the end".

QUOTE AMO

CONTENTS

INTRODUCTION

Marriage is a beautiful union which be enjoy and not manage. If you want and wish for a beautiful marriage, there are some things to do and some ideas to try out in order to enjoy your marraige.

This book gives you the steps by steps guide to achieve a happy marriage.

HOW TO LOVE?

OVE is an intense feeling of deep affection for someone or something. It natural that we expect to be loved back by those that we love but it does not always happen that way.

We do not always recieve love from those that we love however, we can learn to love genuinely. Loving others the right way also

opens way for them to love
us the right way equally.

How do we love the right way?

Firstly, you have to love yourself
because you cannot give
what you do not have. You
have to understand what is self-
love and love yourself first.

◆ ◆ ◆

Self-love is very important because people tend to treat you
the way you treat yourself.   In
whatever that you are doing, always put yourself first, appreciate your body, who you are and
everything that you achieved

and working to accomplish.

Love yourself to the extend that you care about the food that you eat. Pamper yourself whenever you have the opportunity.

By treating yourself with love, helps you to love others the right way and this enables them to love and treat you the right way.

Sometime, when your partner starts to fall out of love for you it is mainly because you have stop loving yourself like before.

You no longer care enough to work out, make heathly food, or tidy your surrounding and as well as practicing self-hygine. These sometimes makes your partner to drift away from you.

I know that busy schedule and having kids can cause you to have little time for yourself. But no matter what may be the case, always make out time for yourself for that is what self-love is all about.

People tend to give you what you give yourself, take you where you take yourself or even buy you what you can buy for youself.

"To fall in love with yourself is the first secret to happiness."

ROBERT MORLEY

MAKE TIME FOR EACH OTHER/HOW

Spending quality time together is one of the most important aspect of having a happy marriage.

Spending time will enable you both to continue to bond and discover more about each other such as their strenghts, weaknesses, what they are going through at work or at home, what they are planning and their set backs and progress.

Knowing much about your partner help you to make the best decision in their interest, what to say and when to say it, how to react over an issue or topic based on how sensitive they are and otherwise.

I know you might be wondering why do you need to spend more time with someone that you live in the same house with and share bed with practically every night.

Yes, you need it. Living in the same house without having just you too moments in your world is just like two flatmate with a touch of friends with benefit.

It is just like social media where you only see the pictures that are accessable to you but not the true state of the situation.

Having just you two moment, enable couples to communcate good, open up more about their worries, real situation of things both positive and negative.

Let me paint a picture of what "You two moment" looks like if you are a bit confuse now.

It is usually planned or scheduled as a routine for a

particaular time or day. You
both prepare for it, you can
call it a date, this date can
happen within the house
or outside the house.

As parents of young kids, it is
expensive to plan outside date
often because we had to pay for
a nanny to take care of the kids.
So what we do is to plan our
date at home Friday and satuar-
day nights each week.

We will get our favourite drinks,
porncorns and some hand foods.
We make sure that kids go to bed
before 8pm . We take our shower
and wear something that will

be attractive to each other.

We can decide to watch movie
a short movie or play some
cool music while we have
some cool discussion.

You do be surprised how open
and free you will be having a discussion at this points. You will
feel young and alive. Most im-
portantly, it feels so good just as
in the begining the relationship.

These dates will give life to
your relationship beyond
what you could imagined.

"Time is the currency of relationships. If you want to invest into your relationships, start by investing your time"

DAVE WILLIS,ORG

After having our kids, together with our career it became difficult to spend quality time together. Ofcourse, we talk and do things together but the fire and attention were fedding away. We give the kids almost all the attentions and hardly give each other.

We began to drift apart and tensions pilling up between us. But since we started our date weekends our relationship has been so beautiful. We are always anticipating our date weekend.

BE GRATEFUL FOR
HAVING EACH OTHER

Appreciation goes a long way to motivates one to do more. Make it a habit to appreciate your partner over every little thing that they do through your actions and speech.

Make them know how much they mean to you as often as possible, this helps to keep love alive. Make them to feel special

even when they are not celebrat-
ing anything, buy gift ramdomly
and just say "thank you for been
in my life, I am grateful and
lucky to have you".

Appreciations like these
makes it easier to love
each other even more.

*"As we express our
gratitude, we must
never forget that the
hightest appreciation*

*is not to utter words,
but to live by them"*

JOHN F. KENNEDY

It is human nature to always want and desire appreciation. Feeling appreciated empowers one to do more.

Just as you desire to be appreciated that is the way your partners desires to be appreciated too.

Showing appreciation is not just by saying it or buying gifts for your partner but what matters the most is that you are very attentive to notice when appreciation is needed and show one accordingly.

When your partner does things around the house dont see it as their responsibilies or feel that this is a man's duty and this is a woman's duty xs. He or her is doing those chores to support and would appreciate if you can help once in a while, acknowlege and appreciate their efforts.

When my partner helps me to do things around the house it makes me feel appreciated, it is not just about the help but it also gladdens my heart for the fact that he noticed that I am busy, tired, need a helping or even a break.

"Let us be grateful to people who make us happy; they are the charming gardeners who make our souls blossom"

MARCEL PROUST

ACCEPT YOUR MISTAKES AND APOLOGIZE

If you really want a happy home, this is the one of major key points. It is very necessary to accept your wrongs and to apologise rather than pushing blames. Pushing blames might work for sometime but not for too long. At a point your partner will start seeing through it and this will cause a denth in your relationship.

Accepting your wrongs and apolpgising shows that you respect and value your partner or your relationship.

"The best apology is simple admitting your mistake. The worst apology is dressing up your mistake with rationalizations to make it look like you were not really at fault

but just misunderstood"

DODINSKY

One thing is to apologise but another is for the apology to be accepted. The manner in which apology is randered also determines if it will be accepted. When you all truly sorry over your wrongs, please accept full responsibility of your actions and apologise wholeheartedly.

Randering an apology is not the end but putting effort to avoid the mistake repeating itself is more important. Repeating the same mistake shows unsenri-ousness and lack of respect to your partnes's feelings.

If you are one that your partner wronged, once they truly apologise please forgive and do not use it against he/her in the future. "A happy marriage is a union of two forgivers"

*Forgiveness to me
does not mean
accepting someone*

apology. It means understanding fully that a person made a mistake but is worthy of a second chance

NISHAN PANWAR

ACKNOWLEDGEMENT

I wish acknowledge the holy spirit, my darling husband and my loving kids for their support.

ABOUT THE AUTHOR

Onyimon

Onyimon is an accountant by profession, she is very passonate writer on marriage, relationship and family topics.

she is a wife and a mother of three lovely boys.

www.ingramcontent.com/pod-product-compliance
Lightning Source LLC
Chambersburg PA
CBHW061327140726
47998CB00007B/2590